I0426238

Evaluation of the Sensitivity of Inventory and Monitoring National Parks to Nutrient Enrichment Effects from Atmospheric Nitrogen Deposition

Southern Colorado Plateau Network (SCPN)

Natural Resource Report NPS/NRPC/ARD/NRR—2011/330

T. J. Sullivan
T. C. McDonnell
G. T. McPherson
S. D. Mackey
D. Moore

E&S Environmental Chemistry, Inc.
P.O. Box 609
Corvallis, OR 97339

February 2011

U.S. Department of the Interior
National Park Service
Natural Resource Program Center
Denver, Colorado

The National Park Service, Natural Resource Program Center publishes a range of reports that address natural resource topics of interest and applicability to a broad audience in the National Park Service and others in natural resource management, including scientists, conservation and environmental constituencies, and the public.

The Natural Resource Report Series is used to disseminate high-priority, current natural resource management information with managerial application. The series targets a general, diverse audience, and may contain NPS policy considerations or address sensitive issues of management applicability.

All manuscripts in the series receive the appropriate level of peer review to ensure that the information is scientifically credible, technically accurate, appropriately written for the intended audience, and designed and published in a professional manner.

This report received peer review by subject-matter experts who were not directly involved in the collection, analysis, or reporting of the data. Data in this report were collected and analyzed using methods based on established, peer-reviewed protocols and were analyzed and interpreted within the guidelines of the protocols.

Views, statements, findings, conclusions, recommendations, and data in this report do not necessarily reflect views and policies of the National Park Service, U.S. Department of the Interior. Mention of trade names or commercial products does not constitute endorsement or recommendation for use by the U.S. Government.

This report is available from Air Resources Division of the NPS (http://www.nature.nps.gov/air/Permits/ARIS/networks/n-sensitivity.cfm) and the Natural Resource Publications Management website (http://www.nature.nps.gov/publications/nrpm/).

Please cite this publication as:

Sullivan, T. J., T. C. McDonnell, G. T. McPherson, S. D. Mackey, and D. Moore. 2011. Evaluation of the sensitivity of inventory and monitoring national parks to nutrient enrichment effects from atmospheric nitrogen deposition: Southern Colorado Plateau Network (SCPN). Natural Resource Report NPS/NRPC/ARD/NRR—2011/330. National Park Service, Denver, Colorado.

NPS 960/106694, February 2011

Southern Colorado Plateau Network (SCPN)

National maps of atmospheric N emissions and deposition are provided in Maps A and B as context for subsequent network data presentations. Map A shows county level emissions of total N for the year 2002. Map B shows total N deposition, again for the year 2002.

There are five parks in the Southern Colorado Plateau Network that are larger than 100 square miles: Canyon de Chelly (CACH), El Malpais (ELMA), Glen Canyon (GLCA), Grand Canyon (GRCA), and Petrified Forest (PEFO). In addition, there are 14 smaller parks.

Total annual N emissions, by county, are shown in Map C for lands in and surrounding the Southern Colorado Plateau Network. County-level emissions within the network ranged from less than 1 ton per square mile to between 5 and 20 tons per square mile. In general, annual county N emissions were less than 5 tons per square mile throughout most of the network. Point source emissions of oxidized (nitrogen oxides, NO_x) and reduced (ammonia, NH_3) N are shown in Map D. There are several very large (larger than 5,000 tons per square mile) point sources of oxidized N in this network. Urban centers within the network and within a 300 mile buffer around the network are shown in Map E. There are few human population centers within the network; only one is larger than 100,000 people.

Total N deposition in and around the network is shown in Map F. Included in this analysis are both wet and dry forms of N deposition and both the oxidized and reduced N species. Total N deposition within the network ranged from less than 2 kg N/ha/yr to between 2 and 5 kg N/ha/yr. The majority of the network receives estimated total N deposition between 2 and 5 kg N/ha/yr.

Land cover in and around the network is shown in Map G. The predominant cover types within this network are generally shrubland, forest, and grassland/herbaceous.

Map H shows the distribution within the parks that occur in this network of the five vegetation types thought to be most responsive to nutrient N enrichment effects (arctic, alpine, grassland and meadow, wetland, and arid and semi-arid). In general, the predominant sensitive vegetation type within these parks is arid and semi-arid.

Park lands requiring special protection against potential adverse impacts associated with nutrient N enrichment from atmospheric N deposition are shown in Map I. Also shown on Map I are all federal lands designated as wilderness, both lands managed by NPS and also lands managed by other federal agencies. The land designations used to identify this heightened protection included Class I designation under the CAAA and wilderness designation. There are considerable areas within this network designated as wilderness and Class I. GRCA and PEFO are both Class I. Most of the designated wilderness area is outside NPS jurisdiction.

Network rankings are given in Figures A through C as the average ranking of the Pollutant Exposure, Ecosystem Sensitivity, and Park Protection metrics, respectively. Figure D shows the overall network Summary Risk ranking. In each figure, the rank for this particular network is highlighted to show its relative position compared with the ranks of the other 31 networks.

The Southern Colorado Plateau Network ranks in the lowest quintile, among networks, in N pollutant Exposure (Figure A). Nitrogen emissions and N deposition within the network are both low. However, the network Ecosystem Sensitivity ranking is Very High, within the highest quintile among networks (Figure B). This is mainly because there is substantial vegetation coverage in the I&M parks that occur in this network that include vegetation types expected to be especially sensitive to nutrient enrichment effects from N deposition. This network ranks at the bottom of the third quintile in Park Protection, having only moderate amounts of protected lands (Figure C).

In combination, the network rankings for Pollutant Exposure, Ecosystem Sensitivity, and Park Protection yield an overall Network Risk ranking that is near the median, in the middle quintile among all networks (Figure D). The overall level of concern for nutrient N enrichment effects on I&M parks within this network is considered Moderate.

Similarly, park rankings are given in Figures E through H for the same metrics. In the case of the park rankings, we only show in the figures the parks that are larger than 100 square miles. Relative ranks for all parks, including the smaller parks, are given in Table A and Appendix B. As for the network ranking figures, the park ranking figures highlight those parks that occur in this network to show their relative position compared with parks in the other 31 networks. Note that the rankings shown in Figures E through H reflect the rank of a given park compared with all other parks, irrespective of size.

The five I&M parks within the Southern Colorado Plateau Network that are larger than 100 square miles are all ranked in the lowest or second lowest quintile among parks in Pollutant Exposure (Figure E). Similarly, all of the smaller parks, except Aztec Ruins (AZRU, which is ranked in the middle quintile), were ranked in one of the two lowest quintiles for Pollutant Exposure. Ecosystem Sensitivity is relatively high, within the two highest quintiles among parks for three of the larger parks: GLCA, GRCA, and PEFO (Figure F) and 11 of the smaller parks (Table A). Four of the large parks are ranked in the highest (GRCA, PEPO) or second highest (ELMA, GLCA) quintile for Park Protection (Figure G). Most (12 of 14) smaller parks are ranked in the middle quintile for Park Protection.

Overall, the Summary Park Risk ranking is in the highest quintile among parks for two of the large parks (GRCA, PEFO) and one of the smaller parks (Mesa Verde, MEVE; Figure H, Table A). Most of the other parks (including CACH, ELMA, and GLCA) are ranked lower, in the lowest to middle quintiles.

Table A. Relative rankings of individual I&M parks within the network for Pollutant Exposure, Ecosystem Sensitivity, Park Protection, and Summary Risk from atmospheric nutrient N enrichment.

I&M Parks[2] in Network	Relative Ranking of Individual Parks[1]			
	Pollutant Exposure	Ecosystem Sensitivity	Park Protection	Summary Risk
Aztec Ruins	Moderate	High	Moderate	Low
Bandelier	Low	High	Very High	High
Canyon de Chelly	Low	Moderate	Moderate	Very Low
Chaco Culture	Low	Very High	Moderate	Low
El Malpais	Low	Low	High	Low
El Morro	Low	High	Moderate	Very Low
Glen Canyon	Very Low	High	High	Moderate
Grand Canyon	Very Low	Very High	Very High	Very High
Hubbell Trading Post	Low	Moderate	Moderate	Very Low
Mesa Verde	Low	High	Very High	Very High
Navajo	Very Low	Moderate	Moderate	Very Low
Petrified Forest	Low	Very High	Very High	Very High
Petroglyph	Low	Very High	Moderate	Low
Rainbow Bridge	Very Low	High	Moderate	Very Low
Salinas Pueblo Missions	Very Low	Very High	Moderate	Low
Sunset Crater Volcano	Low	Low	Moderate	Very Low
Walnut Canyon	Low	High	Moderate	Low
Wupatki	Very Low	High	Moderate	Very Low
Yucca House	Low	High	Moderate	Low

[1] Relative park rankings are designated according to quintile ranking, among all I&M Parks, from the lowest quintile (very low risk) to the highest quintile (very high risk).

[2] Park name is printed in bold italic for parks larger than 100 square miles.

Map A.   National map of total N emissions by county for the year 2002. Both oxidized (nitrogen oxides, NO_x) and reduced (ammonia, NH_3) forms of N are included. The total is expressed in tons per square mile per year. (Source of data: EPA National Emissions Inventory, http://www.epa.gov/ttn/chief/net/2002inventory.html)

Map B.   Total N deposition for the conterminous United States for the year 2002, expressed in units of kilograms of N deposited from the atmosphere to the earth surface per hectare per year. Wet and dry forms of both oxidized (nitrogen oxides, NO_x) and reduced (ammonia, NH_3) N are included. For the eastern half of the country, wet deposition values were derived from interpolated measured values from NADP (three-year average centered on 2002) and dry deposition values were derived from 12-km CMAQ model projections for 2002. For the western half of the country, both wet and dry deposition values were derived from 36-km CMAQ model projections for 2002. NADP interpolations were performed using the approach of Grimm and Lynch (1997). CMAQ model projections were provided by Robin Dennis, U.S. EPA.

Map C.   Total N emissions by county for lands surrounding the network, expressed as tons of N emitted into the atmosphere per square mile per year. The total includes both oxidized (nitrogen oxides, NO_x) and reduced (ammonia, NH_3) N. (Source of data: EPA National Emissions Inventory, http://www.epa.gov/ttn/chief/net/2002inventory.html)

Map D.   Major point source emissions of oxidized (nitrogen oxides, NO_x) and reduced (ammonia, NH_3) N in and around the network. The base of each vertical bar is positioned in the map at the approximate location of the source. The height of the bar is proportional to the magnitude of the source. (Source of data: EPA National Emissions Inventory, http://www.epa.gov/ttn/chief/net/2002inventory.html)

Map E.   Urban centers having more than 10,000 people within the network and within a 300-mile buffer around the perimeter of the network. (Source of data: U.S. Census 2000)

Map F.   Total N deposition in and around the network. Included in the total are wet plus dry forms of both oxidized (nitrogen oxides, NO_x) and reduced (ammonia, NH_3) N. Values are expressed as kilograms of N deposited per hectare per year. (Source of data: CMAQ Model wet and dry deposition data for 2002; see information for Map B above for details)

Map G.   Land cover types in and around the network, based on the National Land Cover dataset. (Source of data: National Land Cover Dataset, http://www.mrlc.gov/nlcd_multizone_map.php)

Map H.   Distribution within the larger parks that occur in this network of the five terrestrial vegetation types thought to be most sensitive to N-nutrient enrichment effects: arctic, alpine, meadow, wetland, and arid and semi-arid. (Source of data: See Appendix A)

Map I.   Lands within the network that are classified as Class I or wilderness area. (Source of data: USGS 2005 [National Atlas; http://nationalatlas.gov] and NPS)

Figure A.   Network rankings for Pollutant Exposure, calculated as the average of scores for all Pollutant Exposure variables.

Figure B.   Network rankings for Ecosystem Sensitivity, calculated as the average of scores for all Ecosystem Sensitivity variables.

Figure C.   Network rankings for Park Protection, calculated as the average of scores for all Park Protection variables.

Figure D.   Network Summary Risk ranking, calculated as the sum of the averages of the scores for Pollutant Exposure, Ecosystem Sensitivity, and Park Protection.

Figure E.   Park rankings for Pollutant Exposure for all parks larger than 100 square miles. Ranks for each park were calculated relative to all parks, regardless of size, as the average of scores for all Pollutant Exposure variables.

Figure F.   Park rankings for Ecosystem Sensitivity for all parks larger than 100 square miles. Ranks for each park were calculated relative to all parks, regardless of size, as the average of scores for all Ecosystem Sensitivity variables.

Figure G.   Park rankings for Park Protection for all parks larger than 100 square miles. Ranks for each park were calculated relative to all parks, regardless of size, as the average of scores for all Park Protection variables.

Figure H.   Park rankings for Summary Risk for all parks larger than 100 square miles. Ranks for each park were calculated relative to all parks, regardless of size, as the average of scores for all Summary Risk variables.

Total Nitrogen Emissions by County
Conterminous U.S.
(tons per sq. mi per year)

Total Nitrogen Emissions
(tons per sq. mi per year)

- Less than 1
- Greater than 1 and up to 5
- Greater than 5 and up to 20
- Greater than 20 and up to 50
- Greater than 50 and up to 100
- Greater than 100 and up to 618
- U.S. States
- NPS Networks
- I & M Parks

Pacific Ocean

CANADA

MEXICO

Atlantic Ocean

Gulf of Mexico

Data Source: National Emissions Inventory (EPA, 2002)
Projection: Lambert Conformal Conic, NAD 1983
Produced for: National Park Service, Air Resources Division, 2010
Prepared by: E&S Environmental Chemistry

0   100   200   300   600 Kilometers
0   200   400 Miles

Map A

Total Nitrogen Deposition Conterminous U.S.
[kg/ha/yr]

Total Nitrogen Deposition
(kg/ha/yr)

- < 2.0
- 2 - 5
- 5 - 10
- 10 - 15
- 15 - 20
- 20 - 30
- 30 - 63.5
- U.S. States
- NPS Networks
- ★ I & M Parks

Data Source: Interpolated NADP Wet and CMAQ Model Dry Deposition for 2002
Projection: Lambert Conformal Conic, NAD 1983
Produced for: National Park Service, Air Resources Division, 2010
Prepared by: E&S Environmental Chemistry

0 100 200 300 400 Miles

0 300 600 Kilometers

Map B

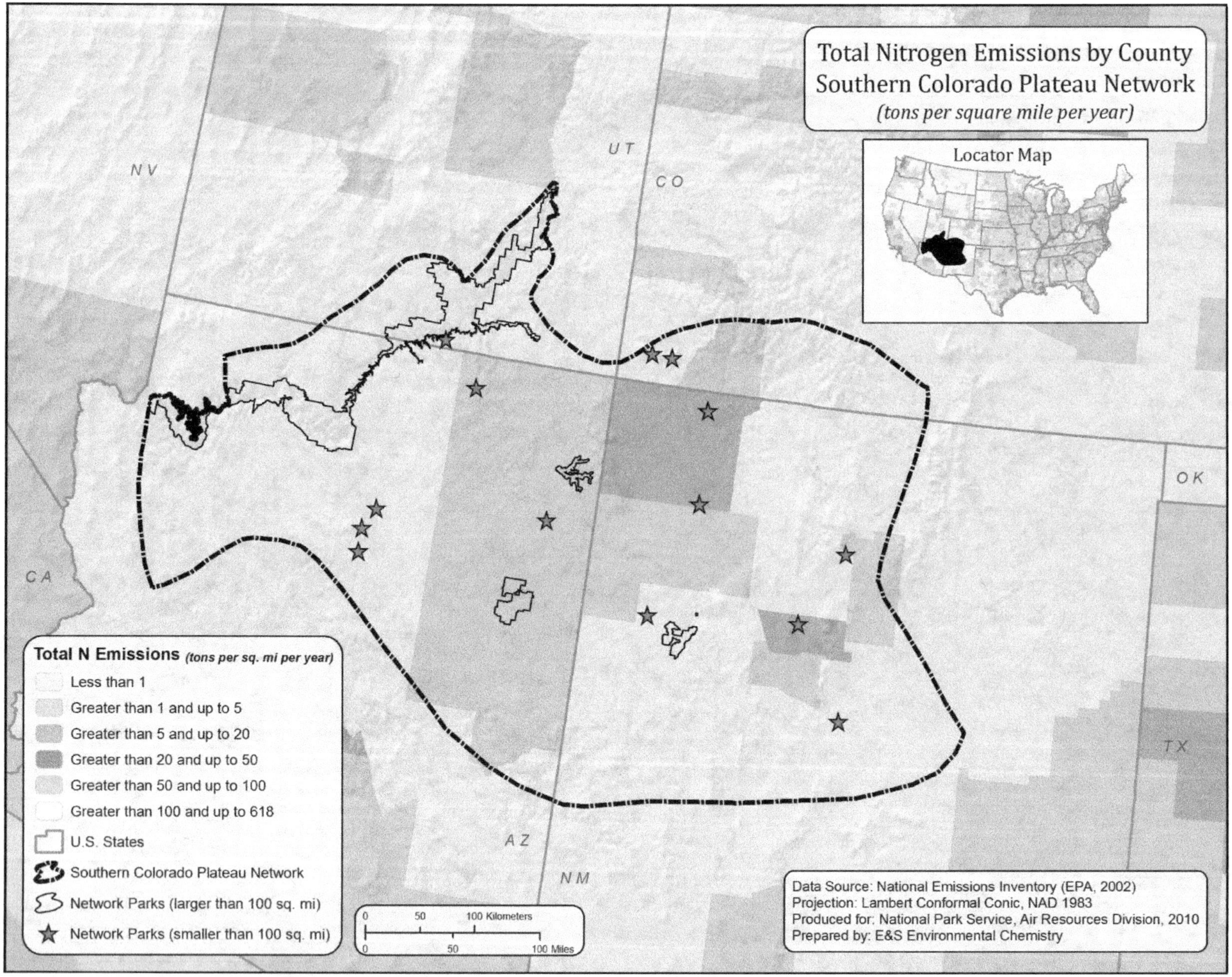
Total Nitrogen Emissions by County
Southern Colorado Plateau Network
(tons per square mile per year)
Locator Map
NV
UT
CO
CA
AZ
NM
OK
TX
Total N Emissions (tons per sq. mi per year)
Less than 1
Greater than 1 and up to 5
Greater than 5 and up to 20
Greater than 20 and up to 50
Greater than 50 and up to 100
Greater than 100 and up to 618
U.S. States
Southern Colorado Plateau Network
Network Parks (larger than 100 sq. mi)
Network Parks (smaller than 100 sq. mi)
0 50 100 Kilometers
0 50 100 Miles
Data Source: National Emissions Inventory (EPA, 2002)
Projection: Lambert Conformal Conic, NAD 1983
Produced for: National Park Service, Air Resources Division, 2010
Prepared by: E&S Environmental Chemistry

Map C

NOₓ (Nitrogen Oxides) and NH₃
(Ammonia) Point Sources
Southern Colorado Plateau Network
(tons N per year)

Locator Map

NOₓ Point Sources *(tons N per year)*
— 2,500 tons N/year

NH₃ Point Sources *(tons N per year)*
— 1,000 tons N/year

☐ U.S. States

⬡ Southern Colorado Plateau Network

⬡ Network Parks (larger than 100 sq. mi)

★ Network Parks (smaller than 100 sq. mi)

Data Source: National Emissions Inventory (EPA, 2002)
Projection: Lambert Conformal Conic, NAD 1983
Produced for: National Park Service, Air Resources Division, 2010
Prepared by: E&S Environmental Chemistry

0   50   100   150   200 Miles
0   100   200 Kilometers

Pacific Ocean

Map D

Park Locations and Urban Centers
Southern Colorado Plateau Network
(Population Centers Over 10,000)

Locator Map

Aztec Ruins
Chaco Culture
Bandalier
Petroglyph
Salinas Pueblo Missions
Canyon de Chelly
Yucca House
Mesa Verde
Denver
El Paso
Glen Canyon
Rainbow Bridge
Navajo
Grand Canyon
Wupatki
Sunset Crater Volcano
Walnut Canyon
Hubbell Trading Post
Petrified Forest
El Morro
El Malpais
Phoenix
Los Angeles
San Diego

SD
NE
KS
WY
CO
NM
TX
ID
UT
NV
AZ
CA
OR
MEXICO
El Paso

Pacific Ocean

Major Cities
- ● Over 1,000,000
- ● 500,000 - 1,000,000
- ● 100,000 - 500,000
- ○ 50,000 - 100,000
- ○ 25,000 - 50,000
- · 10,000 - 25,000
- ▢ U.S. States
- ▢ 300 Mile Network Buffer
- ⬡ Southern Colorado Plateau Network
- ⬡ Network Parks (larger than 100 sq. mi)
- ★ Network Parks (smaller than 100 sq. mi)

Scale:
0   100   200 Kilometers
0   50   100   150   200 Miles

Data Source: U.S. Census Data, 2000
Projection: Lambert Conformal Conic, NAD 1983
Produced for: National Park Service, Air Resources Division, 2010
Prepared by: E&S Environmental Chemistry

Map E

Total Nitrogen Deposition
Southern Colorado Plateau Network
(kg/ha/yr)

Locator Map

Data Source: CMAQ Model for 2002
Projection: Lambert Conformal Conic, NAD 1983
Produced for: National Park Service, Air Resources Division, 2010
Prepared by: E&S Environmental Chemistry

KS

TX

OK

MEXICO

NM

AZ

CO

UT

NV

CA

Total Nitrogen Deposition
kg/ha/yr

- < 2.0
- 2 - 5
- 5 - 10
- 10 - 15
- 15 - 20
- 20 - 30
- 30 - 63.5
- U.S. States
- Southern Colorado Plateau Network
- ✫ Network Parks (larger than 100 sq. mi)
- ✫ Network Parks (smaller than 100 sq. mi)

0   50   100 Kilometers
0   50   100 Miles

Map F

2001 Land Cover
Southern Colorado Plateau Network
(National Land Cover Data)

Locator Map

Data Source: National Land Cover Data (NLCD, 2001)
Projection: Lambert Conformal Conic, NAD 1983
Produced for: National Park Service, Air Resources Division, 2010
Prepared by: E&S Environmental Chemistry

Open Water
Perennial Ice/Snow
Developed
Barren Land
Forest
Shrub/Scrub
Grassland/Herbaceous
Pasture/Hay
Row Crops
Wetlands
U.S. States
Southern Colorado Plateau Network
Network Parks (larger than 100 sq. mi)
Network Parks (smaller than 100 sq. mi)

0   50   100 Kilometers
0   50   100 Miles

Map G

Sensitive Vegetation by Network
Southern Colorado Plateau Network

Locator Map

Data Source: USFS LANDFIRE Data
Projection: Lambert Conformal Conic, NAD 1983
Produced for: National Park Service, Air Resources Division, 2010
Prepared by: E&S Environmental Chemistry

El Malpais

Canyon de Chelly

Petrified Forest

Glen Canyon

Grand Canyon

UT   CO

AZ   NM

NV

100 Kilometers
0   25   50   75   100 Miles

Vegetation Class
Alpine
Arid and Semi-Arid
Grassland and Meadow
U.S. States
Southern Colorado Plateau Network
Network Parks (larger than 100 sq. mi)
Network Parks (smaller than 100 sq. mi)

Map H

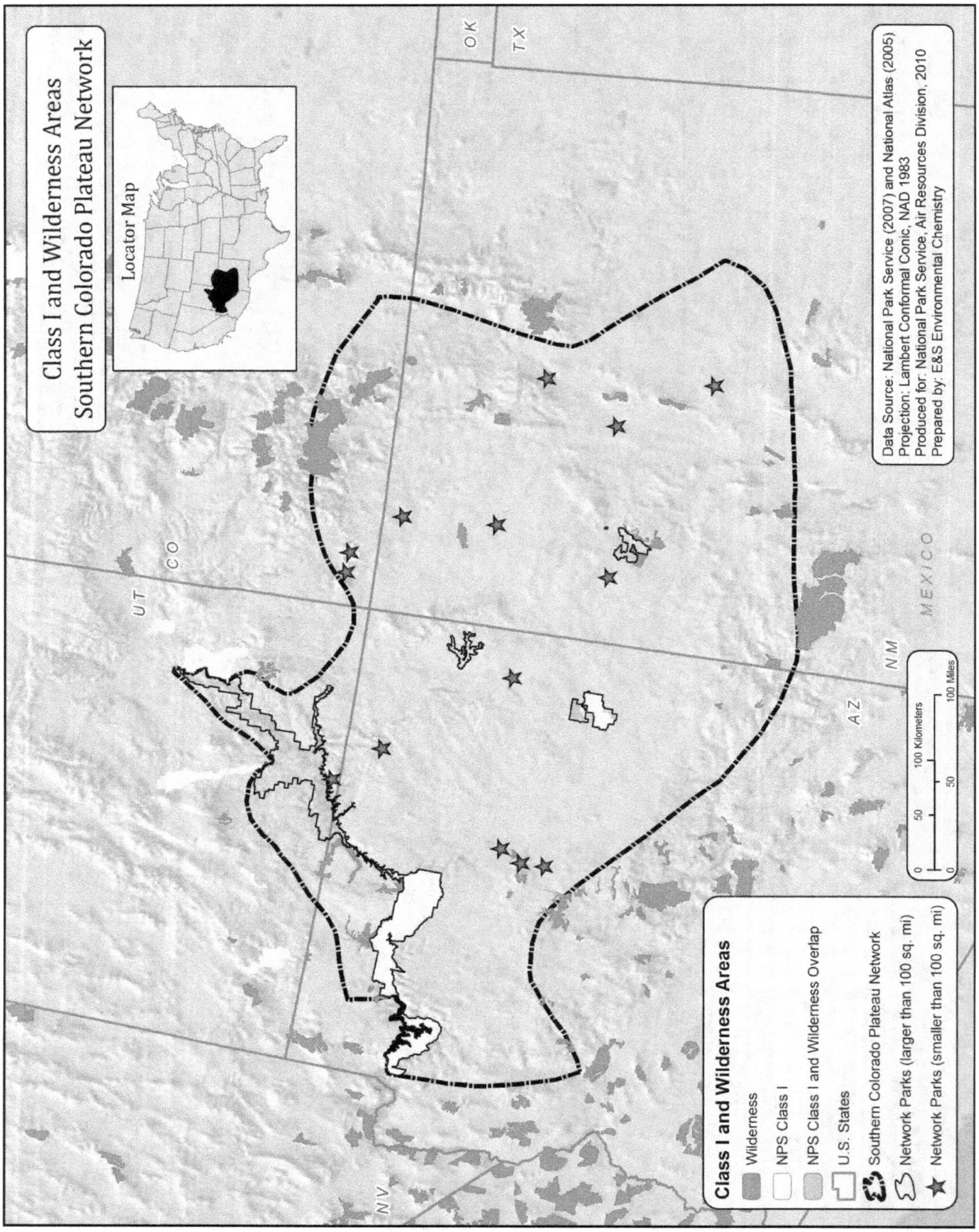
Class I and Wilderness Areas
Southern Colorado Plateau Network
Locator Map
OK
TX
UT
CO
NM
AZ
NV
MEXICO
Data Source: National Park Service (2007) and National Atlas (2005)
Projection: Lambert Conformal Conic, NAD 1983
Produced for: National Park Service, Air Resources Division, 2010
Prepared by: E&S Environmental Chemistry
0 50 100 Kilometers
0 50 100 Miles
Class I and Wilderness Areas
Wilderness
NPS Class I
NPS Class I and Wilderness Overlap
U.S. States
Southern Colorado Plateau Network
Network Parks (larger than 100 sq. mi)
Network Parks (smaller than 100 sq. mi)

Map I

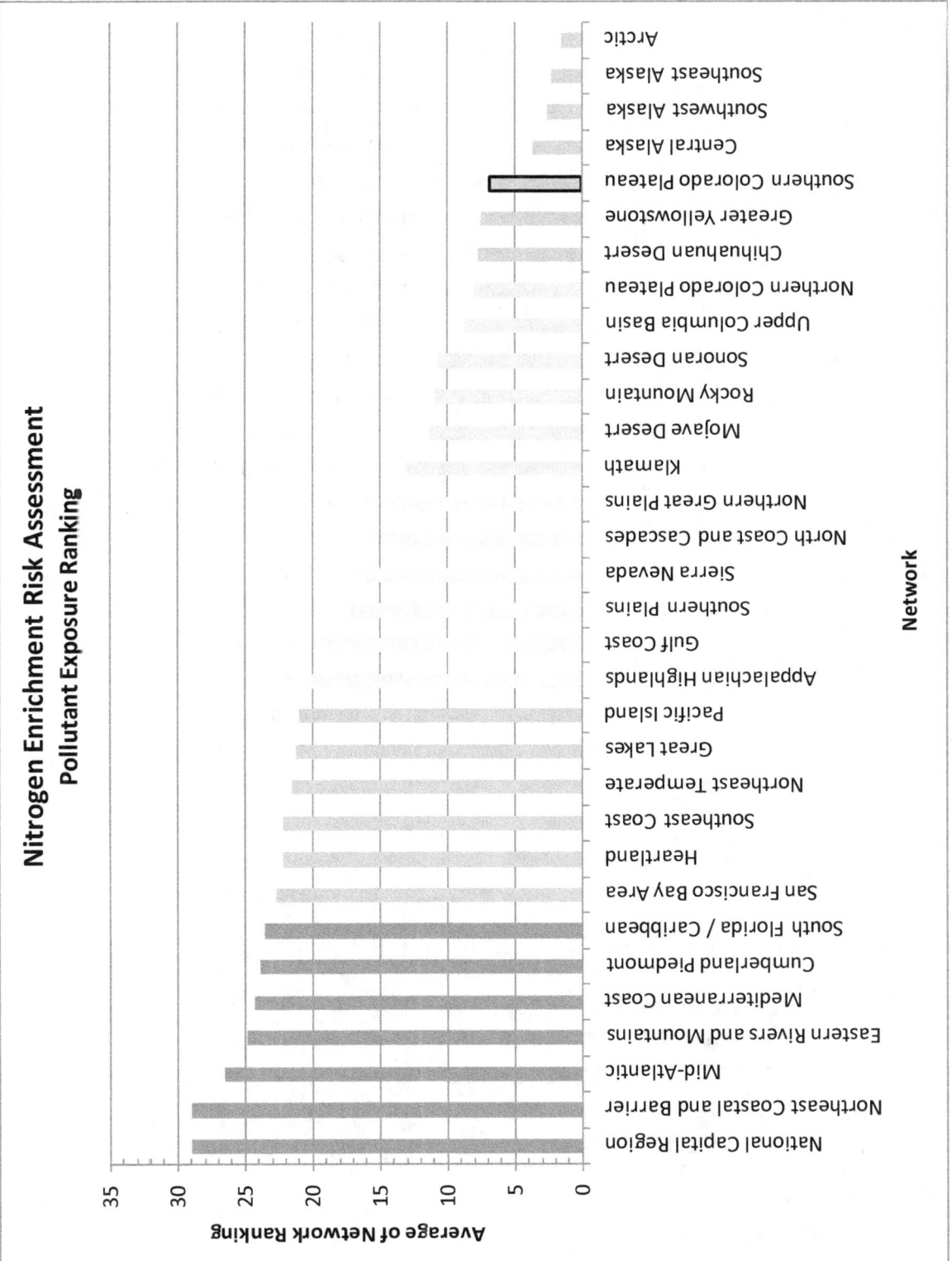

Figure A

Nitrogen Enrichment Risk Assessment
Ecosystem Sensitivity Ranking

Figure B

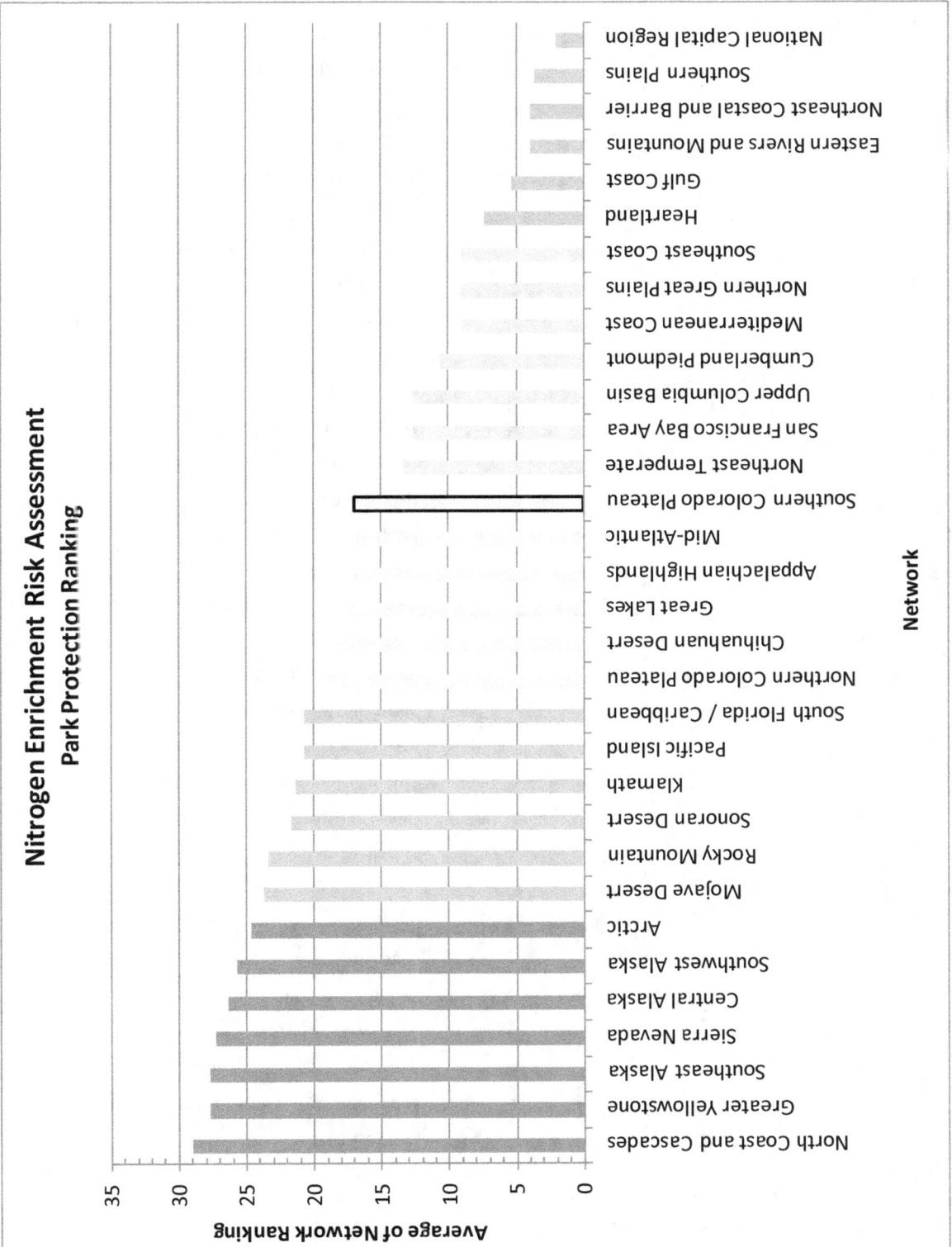

Figure C

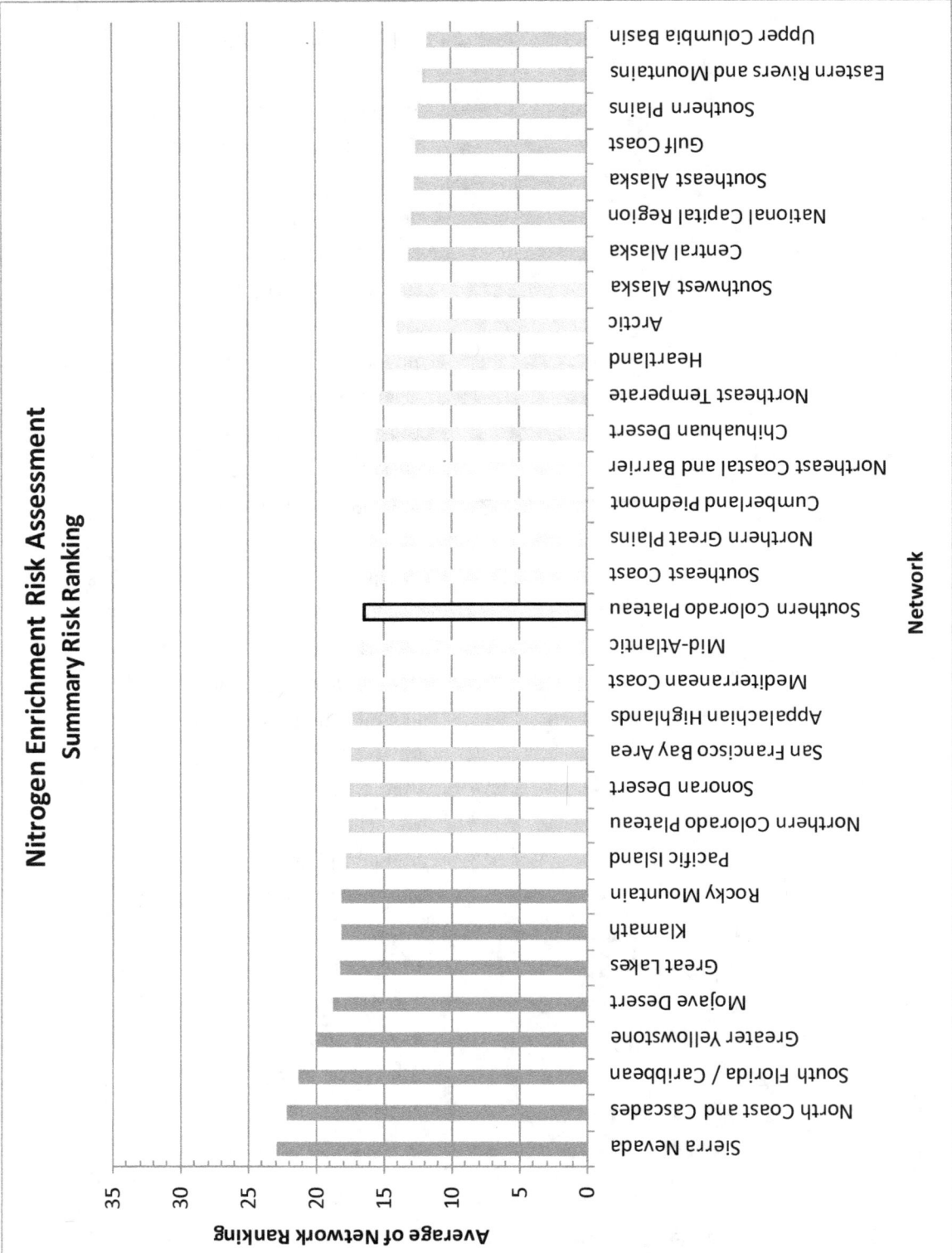

Figure D

Nitrogen Enrichment Risk Assessment

Southern Colorado Plateau Network - Pollutant Exposure Ranking

Figure E

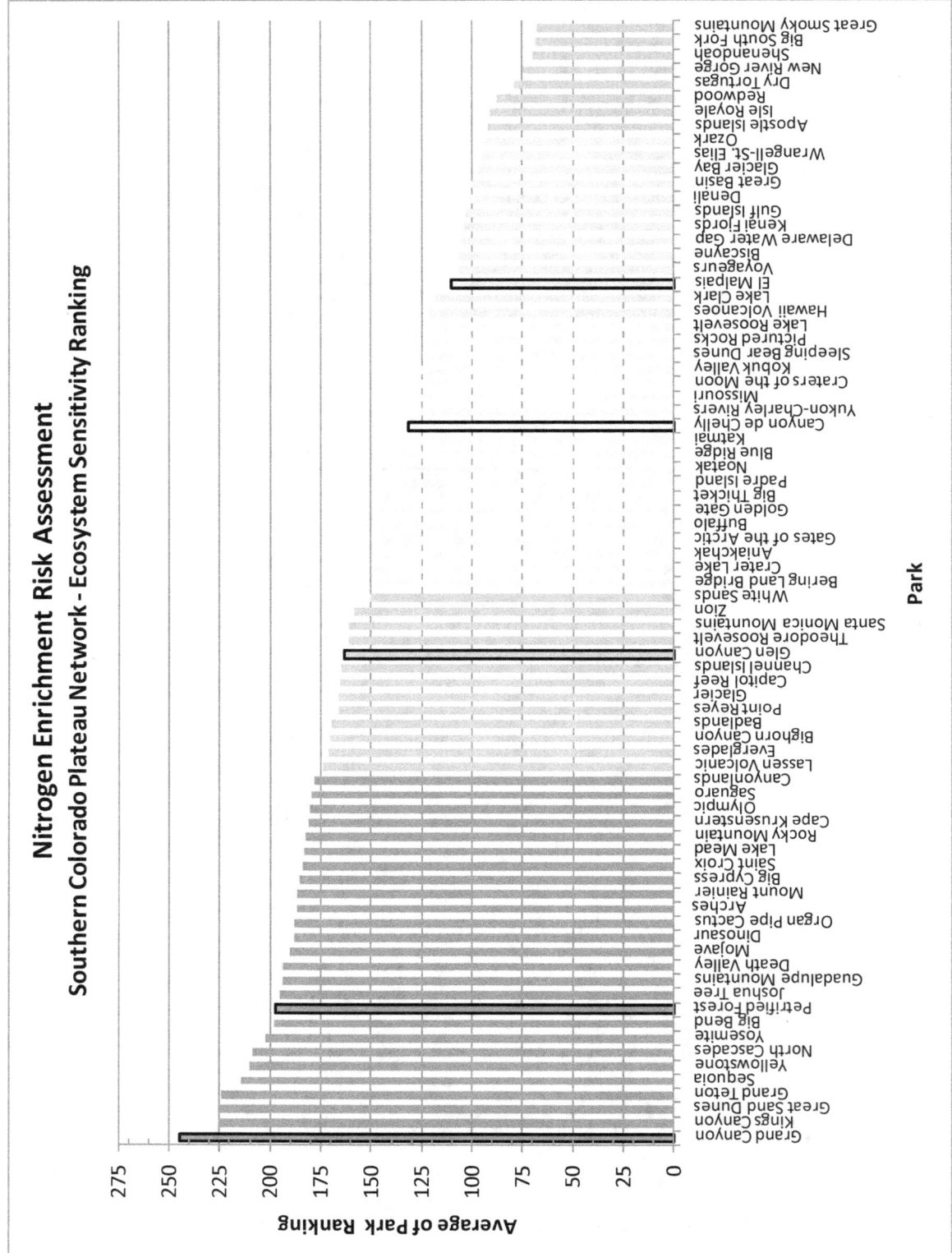

Figure F

Figure G

Figure H

NPS 960/106694, February 2011

National Park Service
U.S. Department of the Interior

Natural Resource Program Center
Air Resources Division
PO Box 25287
Denver, CO 80225

www.nature.nps.gov/air